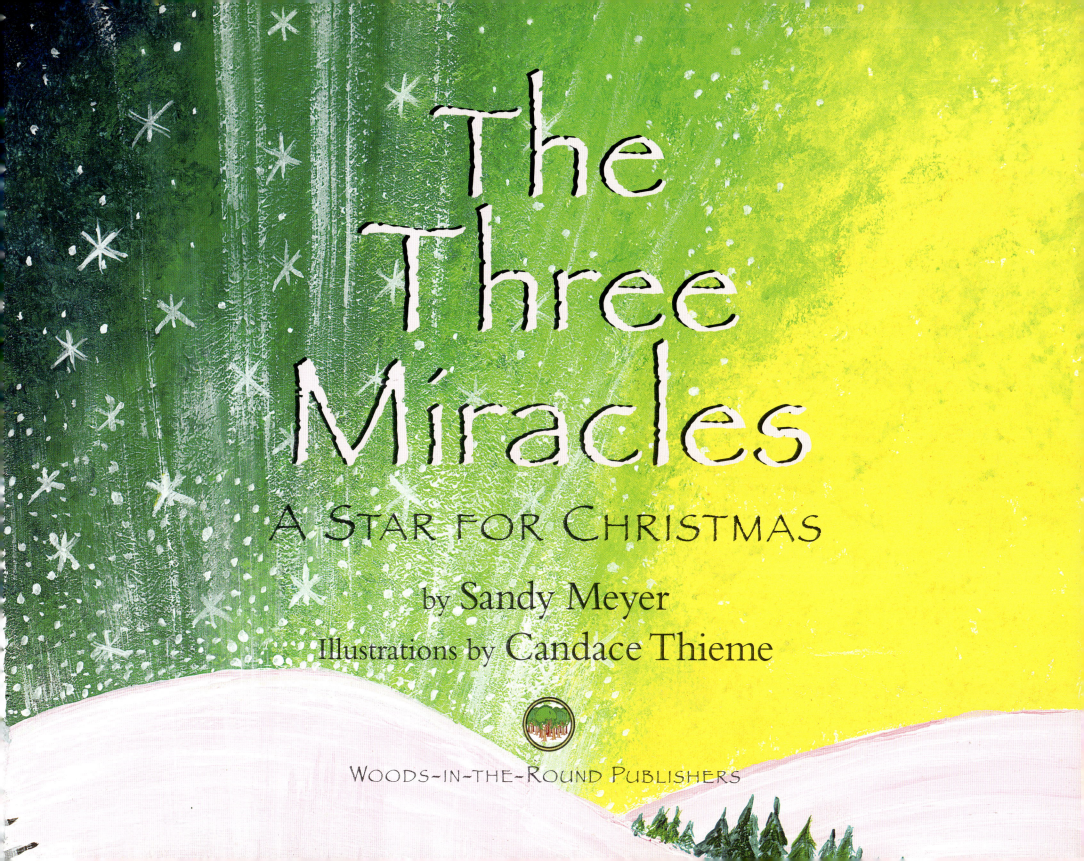

The Three Miracles

A Star for Christmas

by Sandy Meyer

Illustrations by Candace Thieme

WOODS-IN-THE-ROUND PUBLISHERS

To John,

For your belief, support,

faith, and dedication.

Special thanks to Kim Llewellyn for her skill, care, and immeasurable contribution to this book.

THE THREE MIRACLES: A STAR FOR CHRISTMAS.
Copyright © 2008 by Woods-In-the-Round, LLC.
All rights reserved. Printed in China by Toppan Printing. No part of this book may be used or reproduced in any manner whatsoever without written permission except in the case of brief quotations embodied in critical articles and reviews. For information, address Woods-in-the-Round Publishers, P.O. Box 5364, Niceville, FL, 32578.

www.woodsintheround.com

Book design by Kim Llewellyn

Library of Congress Cataloging-in-Publication Data
Meyer, Sandy
    The three miracles : a star for Christmas / Sandy Meyer. —1st ed.
      p.   cm.
    ISBN-13: 978-1-889928-04-3
    ISBN-10:   1-889928-04-6
    I. Title.

Library of Congress Control Number: 2008929129

FIRST EDITION

10 9 8 7 6 5 4 3 2 1

The first snow came late
To the Woods-in-the-Round,
As the very last leaf
Made its way to the ground.
It looked like the snow
Might not come that year,
It was late in December,
The new year was near.

But finally it fell,
The silky, soft, silent stuff,
And by sunset the creatures
All had more than enough.
Yet it snowed and it snowed,
Then it snowed even more,
Till by midnight it covered
Woodchip Woodpecker's door.

Then a clear sky blew in, the stars lit the night,
A perfect combination of darkness and light.
So silent it was, you could hear someone cry,
"Look out below!" from way up in the sky.

Chatter the Squirrel
Was asleep in his tree,
When a bright light flew past him,
And he woke suddenly.
It crashed through the trees,
Then thumped in the snow,
And hissed and sparked
From the snowdrift below.

Just then Jasper the Rabbit
Came hopping by.
He watched the falling light
Leave a trail in the sky.
They stood at the edge
Looking deep in the snow,
And shaded their eyes
From the warm orange glow.

A crowd had soon gathered
At the edge of the hole.
They whispered and pointed,
And wanted to know,
"What is it? Who dropped it?"
"Did it fall from the sky?"
"Will it hurt us?"
"We're frightened!"
The smallest ones cried.

"No, it won't hurt you,"
Came a voice from the trees.
He leaped down in the snow,
Buried up to his knees.
With his hands on his hips,
And a smile on his face,
His red suit bright and cheerful
Brought calm to the place.

Every eye watched in wonder
As he opened his glove,
Tossing up golden stardust,
His greeting of love.
It twinkled and sparkled
As it fell in the snow,
And the light seemed to know him,
And flashed from the hole.

"I have followed that star every year on this day,
  Since the first time it showed kings and shepherds the way.
  This star is my guide on this most special flight,
  Without it, there will be no Christmas tonight!"

"What's wrong with it? Why did it fall from the sky?"
  The little squirrel asked with a tear in his eye.
  "I'm not sure," he replied, "but the problem, I fear,
  Has to do with the way we're behaving down here.

"On that first Christmas night long ago the star blazed,
So bright and beautiful, the world was amazed.
There in the sky above Bethlehem,
It announced the birth of the Savior of man.

"As Jesus lay in a manger,
With no room at the inn,
The animals gathered
To watch over him.
Then the light shined down
On the face of the child,
And the Savior looked up
At the star and He smiled.

"Years passed, then on a day dark as night,
The Savior departed, but He left us his light.
The little star stayed to show us the way,
A reminder of Him on this Christmas day.

"But as each Christmas passed it started to fade,
 As it searched in our hearts for the light that He gave.
 The sad little star weakened year after year,
 Till tonight it just flickered and then disappeared.

"I was just flying past when it fell from the sky,
Now I'm lost with a sleigh full of toys piled high.
If I can't see the way, these toys won't get through,
But I think there's a reason it came here to you."

The rabbit clan gathered and surrounded the light,
They wanted the star and were willing to fight.
"If this star was ours, the rabbits would rule,"
Jasper yelled. "No more biting, those badgers are cruel!"

But the badger gang wanted that star even more,
So they circled and growled, getting ready for war.
They yelled at the rabbits, "Get away from our prize!"
The very small bunnies had fear in their eyes.

The stranger stepped back as they lined up to fight,
Prepared to do battle for the small dying light.
Moving closer and closer, they stood nose to nose,
"It's ours! Give it to us!" the badgers yelled at their foes.

They charged at the rabbits lined up in a row,
They kicked and they bit as they rolled in the snow.

From out of the tree where he'd watched the whole fight,
Chatter jumped to the ground near the flickering light.

"Stop fighting. It's Christmas!" the little squirrel said,
As a flying rock hit him right in the head.

Chatter fell silent, face down in the snow
As the little star gave one last dying glow.
The gangs stopped their fight and gathered around,
The brave little squirrel lay still on the ground.

"It's always the way,"
The stranger sadly recalled,
"The innocent pay
For the worst in us all."
But with faith, there is hope,
And on Christmas Eve,
Miracles will happen
For those who believe.

From out of the shadows came one tiny voice,
His song like an angel, a song of rejoice!
"Silent night, holy night," Pavaratti the Mouse sang,
As his voice strained and squeaked, the first miracle came.

Eight badgers joined in,
And nine rabbits, then more,
The Woods-in-the-Round
Sang like never before.
The badgers on the left,
The rabbits to the right,

They sang of the child
On that first Christmas night,
When shepherds and kings
Were invited to come
To a small, quiet village where
God's work had been done.

The rabbits and badgers
Reached out with their paws,
And made peace with each other,
Pulling in their sharp claws.

The song that they shared
Brought their fight to an end.
They shook hands and were glad
They now could be friends.

"Silent night, holy night, Son of God, love's pure light,"
The animals sang with all of their might.
The second miracle came from out of the dark.
Down in the snow it began with a spark.

The star found its power and roared from below,
Getting hotter and hotter it melted the snow.
Rumbling and crackling it rose from the ground,
Then the last miracle came to the Woods-in-the-Round.

"Ouch! What hit me? Is it Christmas yet? Did I miss it?" Chatter sat up and rubbed his head. "It's a miracle," said Jasper. Chatter blinked his eyes. "We're sorry we hurt you and glad you're alive!"

Whoosh, the star zoomed high above earth,
Brilliantly shining like the night of Christ's birth,
Now the stranger must hurry to finish his flight,
"There's much to be done with what's left of this night."

The crowd clapped and cheered when the star blazed away,
Across the sky galloped eight reindeer and sleigh.
Below they found presents, toys piled so tall,
With a note "Merry Christmas to the best in us all."

The star still shines since that very first year,
Glowing more for the Savior when Christmas is near.
With faith the star will never go dim
When it finds our light, a reflection of Him.